TEACHING READING
to Mentally Retarded Children

TEACHING READING
to Mentally Retarded Children

by JANET K. THOMAS

Publishers T. S. DENISON & COMPANY, INC. *Minneapolis, Minnesota*

Copyright ©, 1968, by

T. S. DENISON & COMPANY, INC.

First Printing—March 1968
Second Printing—July 1968
Third Printing—October 1968
Fourth Printing—April 1969

Printed in the U.S.A.
BY THE BRINGS PRESS

International Copyright Secured

Library of Congress Catalog Card Numebr: 67-31422

INTRODUCTION

As a graduate student, I served as an assistant in a psycho-educational clinic. This experience served as a challenge for diagnosis of a wide array of educational difficulties, particularly in the area of reading. As a group, we were quite well equipped for diagnostics, but not so well versed in remediation techniques. Had Mrs. Thomas' book been available at that time, our clinic would have produced many more "cures." In fact, if this handbook had been at the disposal of teachers in the regular primary grades there would have been no need for so many referrals.

In her unique style, Mrs. Thomas presents a systematic step-by-step program for the teaching of reading. The program is neither totally phonic nor visually oriented. It is an eclectic approach which utilizes the strong points of both techniques in addition to the injection of a good dose of kinesthetics.

The teachers of mentally retarded children will find this fully organized program to be invaluable in their day-by-day endeavors. Each of the developmental skills necessary for reading are separately analyzed and then integrated to the total school program. The teaching materials section of this handbook demonstrates the author's ingenuity, which is a gift limited, unfortunately, to too few teachers.

In a surprisingly small number of pages Mrs. Thomas presents an excellent manual for the teaching of reading. The materials section speaks for itself of the author's inventive genius. This is a must book for all teachers of the mentally retarded and remedial reading teachers; in addition, it should be required reading for cadet teachers in the field. The primary teacher of the regular grades could not help but profit from a perusal of this handbook.

R. J. Capobianco, Ed.D.
Directoral of Behavioral Science
    Research Associate
Department of Special Education
Florida State University

CONTENTS

INTRODUCTION

Reading, the interpretation of written language, evolved into a separate subject area as educators' knowledge of the learning process developed. Now the pendulum of progress is swinging in the other direction and reading instruction is again being incorporated into the language arts program in some of the new team-teaching projects. Regardless of whether it is taught as a separate subject or as a part of language arts, the reading program encompasses a complexity of skills which must be developed before written language becomes a meaningful tool of communication.

Reading Is Necessary

The inability to read written forms of communication cripples an individual in our society and makes him unable to function independently. Without a basic knowledge of the various reading techniques the individual nonreader is unable to use commercial transportation, obtain a vehicle operator's license, obtain gainful employment, or even move about within the individual's environmental life space without endangering himself or others.

As adults, mentally retarded individuals seldom read for pleasure—but for necessity. In either case at least some reading skills must be learned. Reading requires the ability to interpret abstract symbols and patterns in order to gain their full meaning. Reading is necessary for the interpretation of written messages of other individuals. The importance of reading in our civilized culture is second only to the ability to communicate orally.

Reading Essential for All Subjects

Retardation in the development of reading skills results in over-all retardation in scholastic achievement and often in social development. The inability to learn to read is often the first noticed symptom of the educable retarded child in public school classes. Reading has no subject matter of its own. It depends upon the subject matter of all other subjects and life experiences for its content. For this reason the individual must have experience with the meanings of the written symbols he is taught. Visual, auditory, and perceptual senses are required for the developmental use of reading skills. For instance, it is difficult to teach the meaning of visual sensation words such as pretty, red, blue, etc., to a blind individual who has never experienced these sensations.

Although there are many instructional techniques for teaching each specific reading skill, the ability to read is developed through the learning of a sequential skill pattern which progresses in complexity from the concrete to the abstract, and from the simple to the complex. Verbal and auditory skills must appropriately be developed first, and a mental age of understanding must be reached before reading instruction is begun.

Design of Reading Program

The reading program for mentally retarded children is not merely a "watered down" version of the basic reading program used in the regular grades and classrooms. The reading program used in the regular grades and classrooms is not adaptable to most special education classes. The reading program for the mentally retarded must consider the individual characteristics as well as those related to the mentally retarded as a group. It is not enough to say that mental retardation requires the reading program to progress at a slower rate. Retarded children are often capable of developing some reading skills, such as learning sight words, knowledge of names of the letters, matching likenesses and differences, and being able to verbally retell a story in order, long before they are capable of other skills.

Technical skills, such as learning phonetic sounds, sequencing, answering comprehension questions, and learning new words from context clues, may need to be developed much later for the retarded individual than they would be in the normal classroom, for the normal individual.

The special education reading program for retarded children requires a completely different arrangement of skills and skill sequences. This means that the understanding of the context of reading skills and the methodology used to teach them must be thoroughly understood by the special education teacher. Adequate materials at all levels of development are a *must*. This is true not only because the retarded individuals stay at the same intellectual level longer, but because more than one approach to the same skill, at the same level, must often be used before the mentally retarded individual can master use of that skill.

Retarded individuals are usually characterized as having a shorter than average attention span. This seems to be true especially with the younger mentally retarded. The activity-type reading program is most successful with children who have short attention spans. Manipulative devices and machines, cut-and-paste paper lessons, and teaching games are usually used extensively in the early reading program.

Preliminary Steps to Reading

The need for reading skills must be developed in the children before a formal reading program of readiness instruction is begun. Readiness and willingness are not synonymous. No amount of willingness and effort on the part of the retarded child will replace actual maturational readiness to grasp formal reading skills. Formal reading readiness is gradually built into the instructional program. Language arts skills of oral communication are needed before the reading program can begin. Retarded children must have a listening and speaking vocabulary before written words—reading symbols—will have meaning for them.

A mental age (MA) of six years and six months is often used as a criteria for the beginning of the formal readiness program for normal children. As mentioned earlier, some reading skills may be mastered before this age, but other skills require more mental maturity and should not be even attempted before children are intellectually "ready." Mentally retarded children are much older, chronologically, before they arrive at the intellectual readiness stage for a formal full-scale basal reader program.

Curricular Adjustments

Mental retardation requires many curricular adjustments. These adjustments must be made in the reading program content prior to the time it is introduced to the children. The emphasis must be placed on mastery of skills which the individual has the capacity to learn, and which have value to him in everyday life situations. The learner's mental retardation requires individualized organization of the reading skills in accordance with the learners' individual developmental characteristics. To have a developmental curriculum in reading it is necessary to understand the characteristics of retarded children as individuals, and in general, and the development of reading concepts—then to evolve guiding principles which take these characteristics into consideration.

Some instructional adjustments which could be made in the reading curriculum for mentally retarded children include:

1. Greater use of concrete social experiences.

2. Greater use of manipulative materials and devices in the developmental program of learning sight-vocabulary.

3. Wider use of audio-visual equipment to help retarded children grasp the meanings of abstract word symbols.

4. Only one new skill should be introduced at a time—previously learned skills should be used with new skills only at "mastery level" where the child is confident of the other abilities required. For example, when teaching the child to arrange sentences in sequence, no new vocabulary should be used in the sentences.

5. The presentation of new steps in each process or skill should be spread over a long period of time. Practice periods should be short and regularly spaced over a period of time.

6. Use should be made of games and other manipulative devices in order to avoid monotony of repetition during practice sessions and exercises.

7. Mentally retarded children need continual planned review of material already mastered.

8. Whenever possible, the teacher should use only those activities and pages in the texts and workbooks that are not likely to frustrate the children.

9. A readiness program in fundamentals in all reading skills is necessary. New work must be delayed until the necessary skills and understandings of the underlying concepts essential for mastery of each new operation are acquired through planned readiness experiences.

10. Reading skills are learned in accordance with needs, familiarity, and ability to conceive meaning. There must be intent, upon the part of the children, to learn. Experience units in which there is a wide variety of activities help the teacher make assignments within the interest and success levels of the individual children.

11. Teachers of the mentally retarded must regularly observe the children's independent work habits for evidence of difficulty or lack of comprehension.

12. Emphasis should be placed upon diagnosis and evaluation in the initial stages of learning and instruction. Diagnostic tests should be used periodically.

13. Care should be taken to see that children are not practicing errors or faulty work habits and procedures. The teacher must be sure children have complete mastery of each skill before introducing an advanced level of work.

14. Reasonable standards of achievement should be set and adapted to the abilities of the individual learners and their levels and rates of learning. It is important that these standards be maintained and re-evaluated periodically.

The Transfer Method

Mentally retarded children may learn to be proficient in one type of reading, but may be deficient in another. They may develop large sight vocabularies and yet read with little comprehension of the words. Generally speaking, retarded children do better at learning vocabulary than developing word-attack skills. All elements of the phonetic reading program seem to develop slower in mentally retarded children. It is important that every child develops each type of reading ability.

Many research articles point out that there appears to be less transfer of learning among the mentally retarded. The methods and materials used in the reading program should be planned to teach for transfer. The teacher cannot assume mentally retarded children will make associations or reach generalizations without planned extension of experiences.

Selection of Material

The selection of the tests, texts, and workbooks for the reading program is usually the responsibility of the special class teacher. In most school systems the organization of the reading program is determined by the textbook used in the regular grades. Each grade then "covers the book" assigned to that grade level and it is assumed all children benefit equally. This textbook method of instruction does not work well for mentally retarded children. It is very seldom that one textbook series will provide adequately for all members of the special class. Ideally, the teacher should be able to use some of the lessons from many series and levels of books and workbooks. Teacher-made materials and related commercial materials can then be substituted for difficult or abstract work pages. The use of combined materials allows greater flexibility for meeting the needs of mentally retarded children.

Reading is often a cause of much difficulty in other subject areas, for mentally retarded as well as for normal children. Their inability to read may cause sections of tests, texts, and other printed materials to be impractical for them. The best way to quickly determine if the children can read a certain material with understanding is to have them retell in their own words the meaning of what they read. Chances are that if the children cannot explain the meaning of the words, it is, at best, fuzzy or vague in meaning for them.

Eliminate Crutches

Immature habits such as following words with a marker or the fingers, verbalizing while doing silent reading, reading without expression and attention to punctuation, or substituting and omitting words and whole lines, seem to be more prevalent in mentally retarded children than in normal children. The use of "crutches" by the mentally retarded seems more common and continues for longer than in normal classes. The special-class teacher must "sense" when a crutch is no longer useful and insist its use be discontinued. Use beyond utility can cause reduction of skill mastery

and also become the object of ridicule by older children.

Retarded children respond well to straightforward explanations of the use of crutches. Simply pointing out that they are no longer needed, that the children are "growing up," and are not to use them because they will be teased, is often enough motivation to discourage their use.

There are other problems such as fluctuating attention spans, perseveration, left-to-right orientation, perceptual disturbances, visual-motor coordination development, and figure-background confusion, which may all be attributed more often to the mentally retarded, and are of an individual nature. When they are present they will also affect the learning of reading of either normal or retarded individuals.

READING AREAS READINESS

Readiness instruction is the first formal level of instruction in any area of learning. As its name implies, its primary purpose is to prepare the individual learners for instruction in the skill areas of the curriculum. Readiness to learn is based on physical, social, and intellectual stages of development. It is unusual to find children who are equally "ready" in all three areas. Each individual progresses at his own rate in each area. For the mentally retarded, the intellectual readiness level is reached at a slower pace than for normal individuals. This is the reason for the delay of presentation of academic work in special classes for the mentally retarded.

Tests of Readiness

There are many reliable tests of readiness. The descriptions of these tests may be found in the libraries of most teacher-training institutions. Reading readiness tests are used in most public school systems. The advisability of using the same test for the children in classes for the mentally retarded should be discussed by the administrator, the curriculum consultant, and the special-educa-

tion teacher. Some standardized measure of reading readiness should definitely be selected and recommended before the instructional program is begun.

Readiness programs are included in most textbook series. Listening and perceptual skills are developed through: picture reading and interpretation, picture and pattern matching, practice of left-to-right orientations, continuing patterns which develop motor skills, and auditory training through the use of pictures, records, tapes, and stories. Vocabulary development is also an important part of the readiness program as it is the building of the desire to read. The children must be taught that written words represent speech and thoughts of other persons.

Through the use of readiness programs, children are taught the skills needed in the beginning reading program. The readiness phase of instruction is a necessary part of the development of reading skills. Even after formal reading programs are begun, readiness for each new level must be developed. The readiness to learn each new skill must be developed through planned activities.

DEVELOPMENTAL SKILLS

The developmental skills in reading include such things as:

1. Vocabulary development.
2. Use of voice inflection and expression in oral reading.
3. Comprehension—silent and oral.
4. Use of context clues.
5. Understanding of sequence.
6. Selection of the main idea of the story.
7. Recognizing detail.
8. Using punctuation.
9. Basic grammar.
10. Eye movement in silent reading.
11. Phonetic reading and word attack skills (word analysis).
12. Extension and transfer of learning.

All basic reading series include the gradual development of each of these skills. When the teacher of mentally retarded children individualizes the reading program by using more than one series, she must be sure that she does not omit the skills taught.

Reasons for Independent Reading

The basic skills necessary for independent reading are a combination of all the developmental skills listed here. If the learner is not allowed to develop each skill to the maximum of his individual ability, he will always have difficulty interpreting written language. There are some teachers who feel it is unnecessary for them to teach the detailed use of each skill if the children begin to read words orally from the basic reading series. This is reading without thought and regard for content—it should never be considered as progress toward independence. It is more practical for the teacher of mentally retarded children to proceed by stages of growth in each skill, without time limitations, rather than by books or time limits for grade levels with only a certain number of days spent on the instruction of a certain book. The beginning skills level usually requires extensive use of teacher-made materials which meet the individual needs and characteristics of the children in the class.

The experience chart or activity approach to reading has been found most successful in teaching reading to younger mentally retarded children. Chart stories require care in their development. The vocabulary must be guided by the teacher and limited to a functional word list the children are capable of learning. The activities used to follow up each chart-writing lesson should include skills from the prior list of developmental skills.

PHONICS

Phonetic and alphabet instruction have been integrated into the basal reader program in most curriculum guides. It has been found unwise in some situations to teach the "parts" before the "whole" is mastered. Once the children have developed a minimum sight vocabulary, by seeing words written and hearing them pronounced in chart stories, the children should be started in a systematic program of phonetic word-analysis skills. Auditory discrimination training should be refined before the skill of hearing specific sounds is taught.

Careful Use of Phonics Necessary

It must always be remembered that many of the words in our language cannot be analyzed phonetically. The utility of phonics generalizations commonly taught in the primary grades has been proven to be quite low. Most authorities do agree, however, that some phonetic and structural analysis skills must be taught since it is impossible to teach every word that must be learned for individual independence.

Mentally retarded children have even less time than the normal individuals in which to be taught the vocabulary needed for independence in reading. As early as possible the teacher should begin auditory discrimination of rhyming elements. Poetry and nursery rhymes—as well as rhymes written by the class—should be used extensively in the beginning stages of instruction.

Students should be able to use and identify sounds in any position in the word with about eighty per cent (80%) accuracy before new materials are presented. Children may be given words in groups of three which contain the elements to be tested. The students should be able to circle the word or elements pronounced with reasonable (about 80%) accuracy. Additional elements such as "b," "d," "r," "ch," "k," "l," and the short vowel "e" should then be gradually added to any sounds previously taught.

Other consonants and sounds should be added as each new level is mastered. The consonant blends and the digraphs should not generally be taught until long and short vowels can be heard in auditory discrimination lessons. Suffixes and prefixes such as "s," "ing," and "ed" should then be added to one-syllable words and the children should be able to identify the root word and pronounce the new word.

Phonics Instruction

When phonics instruction is used with mentally retarded children it should build on what they have already learned. The use of a basic series of phonics books is a questionable procedure in the special-education class. It is wise to have these materials available as resource aids, but seldom do these preplanned programs meet the individualized need of the special-education class.

A combination of teacher-made materials, chalkboard drills and games, commercial devices, ditto seatwork, and selected workbook pages usually gives the best phonics program for the mentally retarded.

Phonics consists of training three separate senses: auditory, vocal, and visual. This is why rhymes are used extensively in the beginning stages of reading. The visual eye-training of similar parts is a much more complex skill which can only be mastered after the other two skills are used at a subconscious level.

Gradually the sounds of several consonants should be taught through the use of charts and sight words. Pictures may be gathered and each sound used in a variety of lessons. Consonants should be taught first, but the introduction of short vowel sounds should either interrupt or correlate with consonant introduction. For example, if the consonant elements "m," "n," "p," "f," "th," "ng," "sh," and "s," "t," "c" are taught—the short vowels "a" and "i" should be taught also.

Phonics provide a useful tool for learning to read—they should be regarded as such. Teachers should strive to learn as much as possible about the phonetic method of teaching and learning reading. When this is done they will be better able to instruct their students in its use. Consonants, vowels, blends, digraphs, dipthongs, speech sounds, suffixes and prefixes, and all elements of phonetic reading must be thoroughly understood before they can be taught to children.

Before ending any discussion of phonics it should be noted that some normal and some mentally retarded children are simply unable to learn to read using the phonetic methods described here. Other methods should be explored and all methods of instruction tried before resorting to the rote learning-teaching process. That process develops a basic sight-word vocabulary but limits the individual to the vocabulary which can be specifically taught in formal instruction. Little independence is gained in this manner.

INDEPENDENT READING

Independent or silent reading must always be done in materials at a level below the instructional level. Children cannot be expected to independently work at a level which requires the use of skills they have not yet mastered. When the independent reading is from assigned stories in a basic reader the purpose of the reading assignment should be clearly understood by the learner. If the reading is for "pleasure" in a library, or a student-selected book, then the teacher should be sure the vocabulary is controlled and limited to the abilities of the child. It is only to be expected that the children will not maintain attention and good study habits if the material is too difficult for them and is beyond their individual levels of comprehension.

Individualized Reading

Individualized reading is a name for many types of programs. It means many things to many people. Educators seldom agree on the meaning of the term. First of all the term is used here to mean: Any program of reading in which the child reads independently from a selection of books which are "preselected" by the teacher to be within the comprehension level of the learner. It is desirable to help the children learn that books contain pleasurable stories which can be read for pure fun. With the aid of a well-stocked library and any of the numerous children's book clubs, the teacher should be able to locate many books for pleasure reading at all instructional levels.

Colored construction paper bookmarks have been found to be an easy way of identifying the level of books displayed in the room for pleasure-reading selection. For instance, a chart may be put up with the colors—containing cards with the names of the children who may read the books with each colored marker.

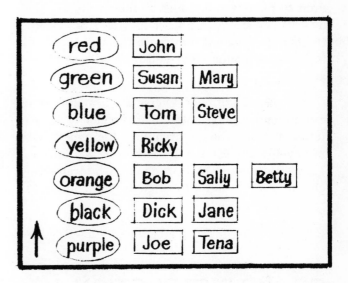

The children may be quickly taught that they may read any books with their colored marker and any books below their color on the chart. According to the example chart, purples are reading at the lowest level and reds at the highest. The books would range from picture books only to approximately the third-grade level. The names may be put on removable cards so children may be moved up or down on the independent reading chart.

Seldom should the children be allowed to read or use books beyond their level of mastery. Only in cases where children have a very keen interest in a certain subject, such as dinosaurs, horses, cars, etc., is it wise to let them attempt to read books which are too difficult for them. It is very easy for them to develop a subconscious attitude that "reading is too hard for me to learn."

CHORAL READING

The use of choral reading in the special-education program for mentally retarded children is a sound practice. Choral reading is a group of two or more persons reading the same material at the same time, in unison. Through reading in unison the shy and unsure child is supported by the other members of the group. Choral reading is usually best done in review material which contains a familiar vocabulary.

Groups of students may read parts of stories responsively or the teacher may ask certain children to read certain pages as they come to them in a review story. In a teacher-pupil situation the teacher may suggest they "read the page together" in a casual manner that will make the child feel at ease.

Many books of choral verse are available from commercial supply houses. These educational materials provide the children with the opportunity to develop a greater appreciation of written language and greater skill in its use. Children enjoy choral reading and will often begin spontaneous responses when familiar rhymes or stories are read aloud to them.

Overcoming Emotional Factors

Choral reading helps mentally retarded children to overcome emotional factors which may block proficiency in oral reading. Also, children with speech defects—often found in special classes—are less self-conscious when reading aloud with a group or another person. Choral reading helps build the ability to read orally in thought units, with good enunciation, and helps to emphasize the importance of attention to punctuation. Reinforcement of vocabulary is also a secondary benefit of frequent choral reading activities.

Whenever possible, a tape recorder should be used in evaluating the effectiveness of choral reading. During the playback, parts can be taken in isolation and evaluated in detail for their good or weak points. This not only helps develop awareness of problems in choral reading, but strengthens the children's ability to objectively evaluate their own efforts.

GROUP INSTRUCTION

Grouping for reading instruction is a basic practice in elementary schools. The special-education class for mentally retarded children presents some unique problems in this respect. The chronological and mental age range is usually much larger in special classes than in the regular classes for each grade. Also, there are fewer children in special classes which means it is likely some children may not be able to be grouped with even one other student in the group. Although this situation is not ideal—it must be anticipated.

Unwise Group Instruction Methods

In some schools the children are sent from the special class to regular grade classrooms for reading because the special class teacher "has too many instructional levels." This practice is usually unwise for several reasons. First, the retarded children would be much older than their reading peers; they would be larger in physical size than the children in the regular grade to which they are sent. Second, the normal class will usually progress at a pace which is faster than the retarded child can handle. Frustrations and emotional problems may result and it may be necessary to frequently place the child into another teacher's room, causing many changing relationships during each school year.

Third, faculty personalities must be carefully considered as some teachers resent having "extra" students placed in their rooms, or resent other teachers being relieved of part of their student load, or prefer not to work with mentally retarded children, or for one reason or another cause friction in the faculty situation because of the student regroupings causing schedule changes, etc.

Fourth, the materials should be carefully evaluated. It has already been pointed out that experience and activity-type methods of instruction are the most suitable for mentally retarded children. In regular grades the textbook method of instruction with only slight variety of method is usually used. All of these factors must be considered before the special class teacher sends her children to regular grade classrooms for reading instruction. She must be *sure* the instruction could not be better handled in the special class situation.

Grouping Children on Same Levels

Occasionally it may be necessary to group children together who are at the same instructional level for group work, but at different instructional levels for independent work. The teacher will find this situation quite easy to cope with if adequate materials are provided. After a group lesson is taught in the basic reader, phonics book, or special skill material, the teacher can assign the independent work of different levels and types to the children according to their individual needs. This eliminates the need for repetition of the group lesson for individual children and saves the precious little instructional time the teacher has for working with the various instructional levels.

Instructional groups should be made flexible enough to include children from other groups when the need arises. The children should be included in group lessons other than their own when material they need is presented to other groups. In a class of fifteen children from (CA) years seven to eleven, approximately four to six reading groups may be needed. The teacher should meet with each of these groups each day, and independent work should be provided for those working at their seats while the teacher is working with other instructional levels. Boardwork, seatwork of ditto materials, workbook pages, and commercial or teacher-made games and devices should be used alternately with those engaged in independent work. All children should clearly understand their directions for work and what is expected of them for the whole reading period. This means as little time as possible is lost in repeating or clarifying directions for the various groups when the work period does begin.

How to Proceed Effectively

It has been found to be a great timesaver if the teacher writes the names of the children under or beside work assigned from the chalkboard. They erase their names when they have completed the assigned work and provide the teacher with a visual check of the children's progress. Games may also be so labeled and work placed on desks so that time is not wasted in getting and returning materials.

As pointed out earlier, many levels of instructional materials are needed in the successful reading program for mentally retarded children. The mentally retarded require short periods of independent work and short formal teaching-learning sessions with the teacher. In some cases it is best and more effective if the teacher is able to work with younger children twice during the instructional period, rather than to present too much new material in one longer session.

Ideally, each child would be taught individually. Since this is not practical, or possible, the teacher should try to arrange her groups to be as homogeneous as possible, and to include all the children who would benefit from them. The special-class teacher usually has the same children for two to six years, depending upon the system's provisions for them. This permits long-range planning and gives the teacher the opportunity to know the children as individuals and to recognize their individual needs.

INDIVIDUALIZED READING AND PROGRAMMED READING

The two terms, "individualized reading" and "programmed reading," have entirely separate meanings. First of all, the term, "programmed reading," will be analyzed in terms of its use in the special education program. Many commercial publishing companies are now producing programmed materials for elementary readers.

Program Types of Materials

These materials are usually in the form of a series of workbook-type books which are consumable and self-checking. Teachers guides are provided and tests are given at various points in the series to be sure the children are mastering the material. Primary-level materials for grades one through three may require as many as fifteen separate workbooks. The one main advantage here is that less time is required for each book to be completed and the children gain a feeling of accomplishment. The familiar grade-level designations of the familiar basic readers are also removed when a program such as this is used in the special class.

Another type of programmed material is produced in *kit* form, with reading and testing materials all color-coded for easing the amount of teacher direction needed. Student pieces are provided and usually printed on gloss tagboard. Additional student materials such as color-coded pencils, answers pads, etc., are consumable. These programmed kits are useful as a supplementary program in the special class situation. Usually these kits do not provide enough material—in either volume or variety—for the mentally retarded child.

Machine Device for Teaching

The teaching machine type of programmed material is the newest and one of the most promising devices for the teaching of reading. Many types of machines and reading programs are available. It would be impossible to even attempt to describe each kind here. Many of these have been tested with groups of mentally retarded children, and a very high success rate has usually been indicated in the final analysis. The mechanical and manipulative aspects of the machines help to stimulate and maintain interest levels while the programs themselves are constructed to restrict the presentation of new material until a sufficient degree of mastery is demonstrated in pupil responses.

Individualized Reading

Individualized reading is not the same as programmed reading—and may, in fact, incorporate programmed materials into the individualized program. All reading programs are individualized to a degree, and truly "individualized" reading instruction as defined by educational dictionaries is seldom seen in the public school situation. Individualization of reading instruction is usually supplementary to a basal reader program in which other materials are used.

Individualized reading utilizes a variety of books, games, materials and devices (either commercial or teacher-made), and machines, in order to present a balanced program suitable to *one* learner's interests, needs, and abilities. Each child would be at a different level, developing a different skill, and working with different materials in the individualized program. The teacher is usually solely responsible for the planning, administration and execution of the individualized plan within the classroom. This type of program requires a great deal of out-of-class preparation time on the part of the teacher and demands that she have extensive knowledge of the teaching and learning of reading methodology.

When a basic-text approach is used, some degree of individualization may still be achieved by incorporating individualized portions of work into the independent work program. Both programmed and individualized reading have definite points of value in the special-education reading program for mentally retarded children. The terms themselves have many meanings to different people, but both are becoming increasingly understood and used in the elementary school reading programs. In the final analysis it is most likely they will both eventually prove to be one more useful tool in the reading instructional program.

HOW DOES MENTAL RETARDATION AFFECT LEARNING TO READ?

The mentally retarded child is most academically handicapped in his ability to learn to read. The ability to learn reading skills is closely linked with individual intellectual development. Since mental retardation actually retards the individual's *rate* of intellectual development and limits the individual's maximum expectancies in all academic areas, it follows that the process of learning reading skills is also limited to the degree of each individual's mental limitations.

Testing by Reading

In the public school situation, the inability to learn reading skills is often one of the first reasons children are referred to psychologists for individual intellectual tests. Through these referrals and the resulting scores, many educable retarded children are identified. When a child's intelligence is such that he is considered to be a trainable retardate, the parents are usually fully aware of the child's limitations and long-range expectancies before he enters school. This is not the case with children who fall into the educable retardate category. Since these children are the upper end of the continuum considered to be mentally retarded, they more nearly approximate the normal individual. Parents are very often unaware of their child's retardation.

Educable retarded children are those whose individual intelligence test scores fall between 50 and 75 or 80 on individual tests of mental ability given by licensed school psychologists. This means that the child's mental age (MA) will be 50 to 75 per cent of his chronological age (CA). The intelligence score is figured as a percentage of the chronological age of each individual.

At age eight the educable mentally retarded child has the approximate learning abilities of a child between the ages of four and six, depending upon his intelligence test score and its reliability. This means that by age 16 (CA) the educable retardate would read on the same level as a normal child between the ages (CA) of eight and twelve.

In elementary school special-education classes, the children are usually between the ages of eight and twelve and seldom read beyond the third-grade level. One must also remember that there may be remedial reading problems which would further limit the children's ability to read, just as there are children with normal intelligence who, for a variety of reasons, become remedial reading cases requiring specialized individual attention. Although special education classes reduce the need for remedial instruction classes in reading and arithmetic, they do not eliminate the need for remedial classes for children with normal intelligence.

THE SCHOOL PROGRAM

The school program for teaching reading to mentally retarded children differs greatly from the basic reading instruction used in most self-contained elementary school classrooms. In the special-education program, children do not complete the "set" number of basal readers with complimentary workbooks in the same period normal children would take to complete these materials. In many special-education programs, no basal reader sequence is adopted. In other programs, readers not used in the regular elementary grades of the same school system are used to avoid grade-level designations. Some special-education programs use the basal reader program supplemented with other texts, materials, and devices.

Reading and the Total School Program

Reading cannot be isolated from the total school program. It must be considered only a part of the educational experience just as it is only a part of life's total pattern. The reading program for the mentally retarded is limited to mastery of skills which are socially useful to mentally retarded individuals. The school program must contribute to the children's mental hygiene by providing for the individual's interests, needs, abilities, and stage of maturity. The reading program must consist of systematically planned experiences which are both realistic and functional. It must contain knowledges, skills and concepts that will have value to these retarded children in later life.

The content of the reading curriculum draws upon all other curricular areas. Reading has no subject matter of its own. The content presented in the written curriculum must provide the necessary flexibility to prepare the mentally retarded individuals to meet the needs of our ever-changing society.

How to Determine Content

In the elementary educable class, few of the children reach the mental age (MA) of eight years. This must be kept in mind when determining the content and gradation of the reading curriculum. Individual differences are recognized in every group — including special classes for the mentally retarded. To teach the school program successfully, the teacher and school personnel should be familiar with the experiential background of all the children in the class. Cumulative records and psychological studies should be contained in a file of academic progress for each child. Duplicate report cards, duplicate conference reports, health data, standardized test results, and any other pertinent information should be available to those who work with these children.

Learning to read is a gradual process of growth which requires professional guidance to insure that the developmental skills are mastered. For the mentally retarded it is a very slow process requiring systematic planning and execution.

In the elementary primary level special class, during the early elementary school period, emphasis is placed upon developing readiness to understand and use the tools of written communication. The children should begin to recognize, use, and master the skills of the readiness program which will prepare them for formal use of the symbols of written language—word reading.

Use of Basic Reading Skills

The intermediate program, or later elementary period, prepares the preadolescent retardate in the use of basic reading skills. The academic achievement range of this group is usually between first and third grade level. At this stage, mentally retarded children often tend to develop a sight vocabulary considerably in advance of their other reading skill achievement levels. When this does occur it is usually the result of mechanically learned sight vocabulary achieved through repetitious drill, TV, or outside forces. These may include: lack of enough teacher direction allowing child to select vocabulary-type materials, home drill and pressures, sibling pressure from other children in the family, and peer pressure of "playing school" with other children. In any case the teacher must be sure all skills are learned and maintained at an equal level of mastery.

The elementary school reading program is always developmental in nature, and is always diversified in methodology. It is not a watered-down basal reader program, but a carefully planned sequence of skills taught in a systematic method of instruction.

INSTRUCTION

The instructional reading program in a special class for mentally retarded children needs to be based on a sound philosophy and a considerable amount of common sense. The basic instructional *pattern* for each child should be described in the written curriculum guide for the special class. The individualization of this pattern should be the responsibility of the teacher, and when applicable, the curriculum coordinator.

Cautions for Teachers

The teacher of mentally retarded children can never take anything for granted. It is never safe to assume the children have mastered the material presented. These children often say they understand or verbalize comprehension when they have not mastered the material. The teacher must not only hold their attention in learning situations, but require them to demonstrate their learnings. It is important that neither the teacher nor the students become discouraged and permit regression of skill development. More than any group of children, the mentally retarded must have the right educational atmosphere in the classroom if they are to have a chance to learn to the maximum of their abilities. These children need a firm but fair discipline in a relaxed atmosphere.

High standards of achievement should be set at an attainable level for all children in the class. Habits of work must be clearly and carefully developed. They should stress accuracy, completion of work, and neatness. It is necessary that mentally retarded children be taught how to work independently so their attention will not be drawn as easily to the activities of other groups working within the room.

How to Hold Attention

The maintenance of attention can be partially achieved by varying the instructional methods used. The units of instruction should be kept small and no new teaching area introduced until the old has been mastered. Drill should be used only after the children have complete understanding of the skills and can use them independently with accuracy. Material that needs to be retaught or reviewed to retain mastery should be made as attractive as possible. Distributed practice of skills for implementation of knowledges and concepts should be assigned only when needed.

Drawing upon the experiences of the children to provide interest is one of the soundest methods of reading instruction. Pupil interest in the topic is of invaluable assistance to the learning process. While attitudes toward reading are of vital importance to all pupils, they are especially important to the mentally retarded. Wanting to learn for a specific purpose is effective in building motivation. Success must follow the children's efforts if interest is going to be maintained.

Children Must Learn to Think

At all levels of reading teaching, the children must be encouraged to think for themselves. The teacher must try to help the children discover interesting ways to use their reading skills. Positive reinforcement, when given in accompaniment with any behavior, increases the possibility of that behavior occurring again. Some forms of reinforcement which have been used successfully with the mentally retarded are gummed stars, seasonal gummed stickers, picture-marking stamps, progress charts with manipulative markers, graphs, and "Good Work" bulletin boards. Consistency in the administration of reinforcement cannot be overemphasized. Each child needs success experiences.

GAMES AND PLAY ACTIVITIES

Use should be made of games and other manipulative instructional devices. These devices give the children something concrete to *do* while they learn. Many of these manipulative materials are described in the materials section of this book. Success experiences with games tend to raise retarded children's hopes and expectancies. These children need to have *fun* while they are learning. Since they have often found previous schooling to be frustrating, learning to read may have been an unpleasant experience, and they are anxious to think of other things. They need new and varied approaches—those associated with pleasure are usually more effective.

Teaching With Games

The teaching of difficult reading skills and vocabulary can often be clinched through the use of games. Parents and teachers have often observed that the desire to succeed in a game or contest, or to master a puzzle, is a powerful incentive to work. Games provide incentive for improving scores and stimulate the learning of skills necessary to attain these higher scores. Experiences which do not push the pupils to advanced levels of performance fail to meet their instructional possibilities.

Two types of games are most commonly used. Those which make a game of standard classroom procedures or activities, and those which are in themselves a game or puzzle. Games teach children cooperation, honesty, and consideration for others while they give experience in reading skill usage and provide recreation. It is hoped that these educational games also provide mentally retarded children with educational activities which may be beneficial to them in their leisure time.

Careful Selection of Games

The teacher must be sure the games are within the abilities of the children. This may mean modifying the formal rules to meet the needs of the pupils. Speed of response should not be stressed in the initial learning stages. It should increase with mastery of the skills the game is designed to teach or reinforce. Games should also provide them with activities in which they can engage with normal children. The directions should be presented in logical order and accompanied with demonstrations. Practice in the actual playing of the game should immediately follow the teaching. Games should appeal to the students, be of suitable complexity and maturity, have social values, have simple rules, be easily scored, involve most of the players most of the time, and have educational purpose.

TEACHING FOR MEANING

It is the job of the special class teacher to direct the children's activities so that they build reading concepts that have meaning and can be used in solving reading problems. Mentally retarded children are better at memory than they are at comprehension.

The basis of teaching for meaning seems simple enough; explanations must be thorough and complete for each new teaching step. However, more is involved. It is necessary that understanding be developed through several explanations in varying situations and at varying times. Normal children may be able to learn with a single introductory lesson, but this is not the case with mentally retarded children. Several presentations are usually necessary.

Practice Is Important

After meaning of words or phrases is developed, the children should take turns using the newly learned skill or vocabulary. Immediate practice is important. The teacher must determine through trial and error which method of instruction is best for the individual children in her class. There is no shortcut for this. Failure on the part of the children is evidence of trial and error with lack of success. It shows that the children have learned something, but not what they were thought to have learned. Instead of being rewarded for their efforts and making progress in positive directions, they are thwarted and make negative progress in failure experiences. The teacher, too, will find her plans thwarted from time to time. She must strive to be calm, patient, and adaptable to the needs of her class.

DAILY WORK SCHEDULES

Daily work schedules should be flexible enough to allow for last-minute changes in plans. The responsiveness of mentally retarded children seems to be related to weather and environmental influences. Since these are unpredictable factors, so is the "mood" of the children. Restlessness may be caused by the weather or something more tangible, such as incidents on the school bus, at home, or on the playground before school opened. It has been found that a short period of activity play before the formal opening of the school-day activities is useful for settling the children down to work. This period gives them the opportunity to talk with friends, play a game, draw, work a puzzle, read a book, play with clay, play in a sand table, easel paint, or finish correcting the previous day's worksheets or book assignments. This activity period is also useful when the children arrive on a staggered schedule. The morning exercises may begin shortly after the last child arrives, or at a specific time which is used consistently every day.

Adjusting the Work Schedule

When mentally retarded children are disturbed by events over which they have no control, the daily work schedule must be revised. Illnesses or births in the family, company in the home, an approaching holiday, all of these and others may affect the mentally retarded children and distract and disturb them in the school situation.

The allotment of periods of work time, substitute teachers, pupil absence, etc., all affect daily work schedules. The developmental characteristics of retarded children dictate the need for flexible work schedules. Although flexible, work schedules must never be suddenly or drastically changed without warning or a simple explanation of the reason. These children have difficulty adapting to change and need the security or familiarity in the schedule of their daily work. They will, however, accept straightforward explanations of changes which are made by the teacher.

READING FOR TRAINABLE RETARDATES

The trainable mentally retarded individual is not expected to function independently in society as an adult. Even though these children may eventually be institutionalized or become wards of the state, county, or city, they need some basic skills which are taught in the elementary school reading program.

Left-to-right orientation is basic in our society, but the ability to use this directional organization is a specifically learned skill. In walking and moving about in society in one's own life space, it is necessary that left-to-right orientation be mastered. Simple games, rhythms, and activity-type play situations are useful in teaching this skill to trainable retardates.

Using Devices

Matching shapes and symbols is a necessary skill for carrying out simple tasks and recognizing likenesses and differences. Since many of the retardates who are classified as trainable are eventually institutionalized, these are usable skills for the trainable individual. In institutions, the laundry, wards, and special areas are often designated by colors, shapes, and symbols. Higher-level trainable retardates may become useful employees or assistants in institutional shops once the ability to recognize, match, and identify shapes, symobls, and colors is mastered.

Picture reading is one form of reading the retarded can master and find useful and enjoyable.

Pictures play an important role in society. Billboards, labels, advertisements, directional signs, food containers, books, etc., all communicate through the visual recognition of pictures. Many of the games and devices in the materials section can be adapted to the reading needs of the trainable retardate. The teacher must be aware of the fact that as many as one hundred presentations of a given word or picture symbol may be necessary before mastery is accomplished. These presentations would be spaced over a long period of time and involve the use of many varied instructional approaches.

The teacher of trainable retarded children deals primarily with language skills rather than reading skills. Only when some degree of proficiency is developed in spoken language can the basic reading skills be taught. When materials are adapted for the trainable child, simplicity of structure, design, and direction must always be kept in mind.

The learning time of the trainable mentally retarded child should never be wasted. Words and symbols which have little or no meaning in later life should be left untaught. Only those skills and topics which will have distinct social value in the individual's life and environment should be included in this basic program. The learning time of the trainable retardate is so short that only necessary skills may be taught.

TEACHING MATERIALS SECTION

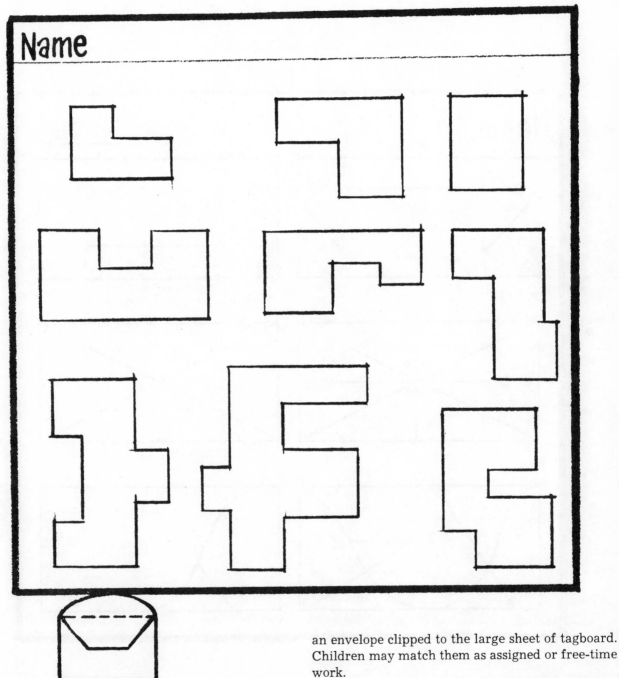

Name

A set of matching shapes is cut from tagboard and then traced on it. The cut pieces are kept in an envelope clipped to the large sheet of tagboard. Children may match them as assigned or free-time work.

Letters may be matched in the same manner.

Two printed copies may be reproduced and one pasted onto the other.

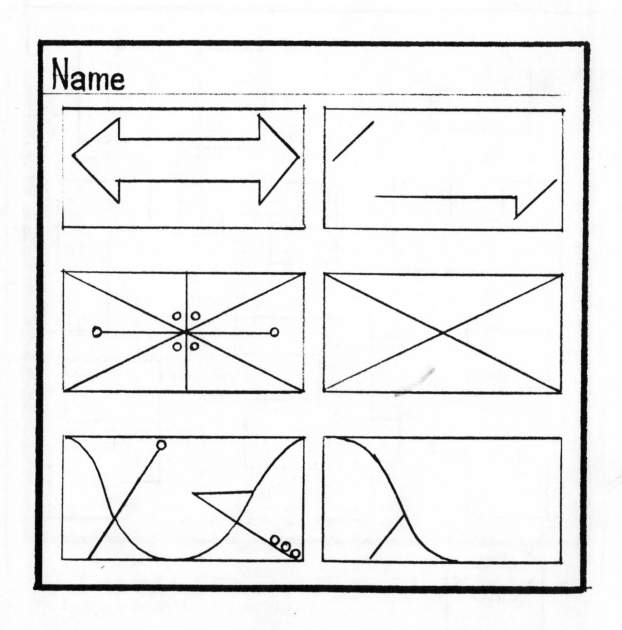

One of the beginning steps in readiness instruction is that of developing visual-motor coordination. Completing pattern designs with a few guidelines to assist them is a good beginning step.

After children are able to reproduce a design with reasonable accuracy when parts are provided for them, plain copying exercises provide the next level of difficulty. Designs may be as simple or complex as necessary.

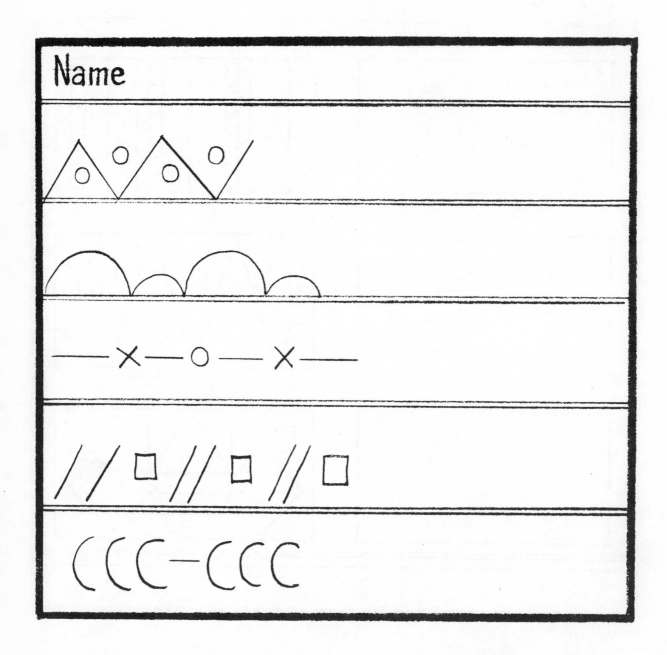

When visual-motor coordination is refined to the point where designs can be accurately copied, the continuation of designs should be introduced. This aids visual-motor development and begins the development of left-to-right orientation.

30

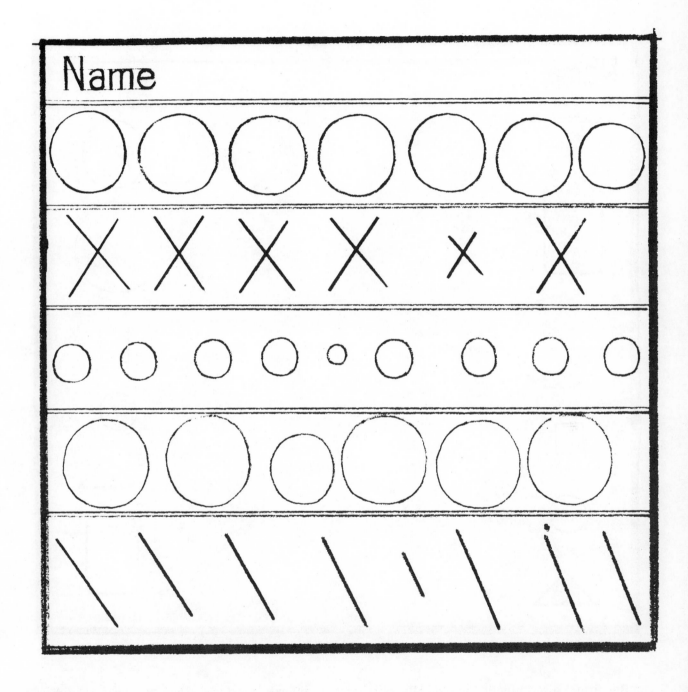

Visual discrimination of size is an important phase of readiness instruction. On exercises such as this, children must find the object in each row that is different from all the others.

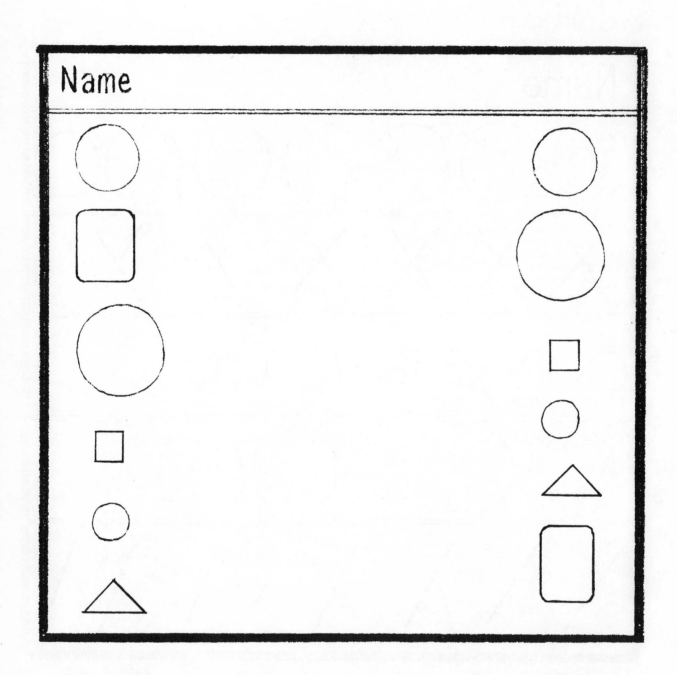

After visual discrimination is partially refined and visual-motor coordination is developed to a degree that lines can be accurately drawn, exercises such as this should be given. Shapes should be quickly mastered, then the level of difficulty increased by matching letter forms, and finally words.

Name

Even before children have developed a sight vocabulary of written words the teacher may begin training the auditory sense to distinguish rhyming sounds.

The child is directed to cross out the whole box if the names of the two pictures do not rhyme. They may be asked to color the ones that do rhyme if the teacher so desires.

33

Name

Name	
1. hat	cup
2. block	**3** three
3. ↑ up	cat
4. tree	plate
5. cake	clock
6. **8** eight	rake
Is this good work?	**Yes No**

This matching lesson utilizes both pictures and words. It may be reproduced on ditto or copied from the chalkboard by the students. The children should say the names of the pictures with the teacher before they begin independent work. This avoids misunderstandings of what they were expected to do and what the pictures are.

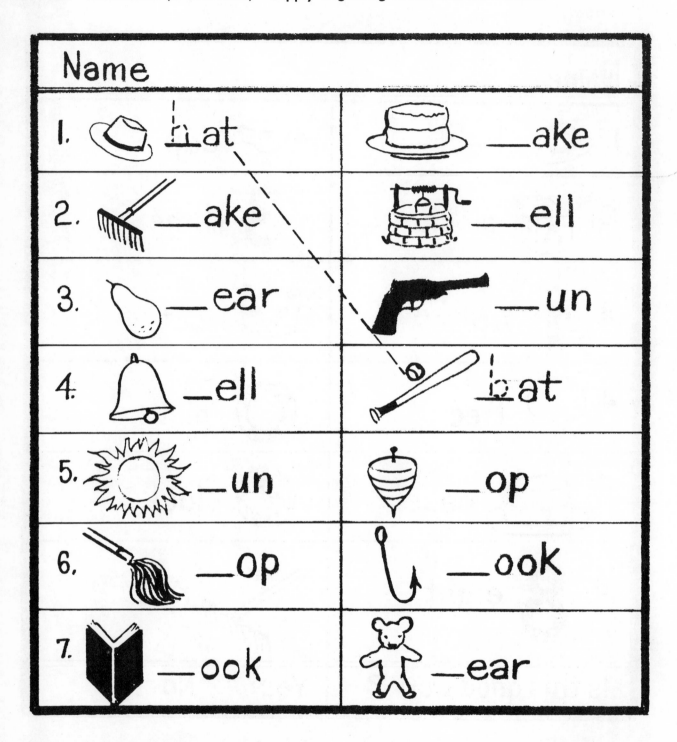

Name

1. __at
2. __ake
3. __ear
4. __ell
5. __un
6. __op
7. __ook

__ake
__ell
__un
__at
__op
__ook
__ear

This rhyming work requires two reading skills. First, the ability to supply initial consonant sounds, and second, the ability to rhyme and match pictures and words.

The lesson may be presented on the chalkboard or on a dittoed worksheet. The pictures should be named to avoid confusion. After the teacher is sure the child or children can identify each picture the work should progress independently.

Name	
1. Cat - bat ?	Yes
2. truck - duck ?	Yes
3. pretty - party ?	Yes
4. down - brown ?	Yes
5. look - book ?	Yes
6. new - now ?	Yes
7. red - read ?	Yes
8. tree - three ?	Yes
9. truck - train ?	Yes
10. ball - fall ?	Yes
11. come - came ?	Yes
12. want - went ?	Yes
13. call - can ?	Yes
14. cake - make ?	Yes
15. house - mouse ?	Yes

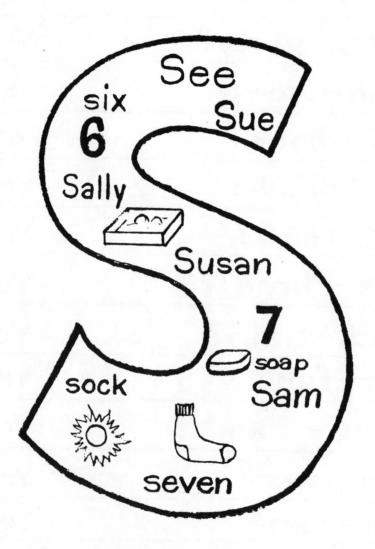

Large letters cut out in the shape of the individual letters are most useful in teaching the initial consonant sounds. The children may find pictures to paste on the outline or write words and draw pictures.

When taken home, these serve as a continual reminder of the sound and are much more useful than the single room chart which is kept in the classroom.

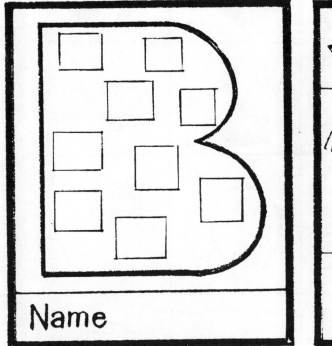 

When first introducing the concept that each letter makes certain and specific sounds, only one sound should be taught at a time. Much auditory training is needed before the children are ready for independent work such as pictured here. They must first be trained to repeat words beginning with the sound. Next, pick out one word from a group of three that does *not* begin with that sound (bell, cat, book). Then the child should think of other words that begin with the sound, while the teacher "prompts" them by making the sound in isolation.

Finally, the children should be able to select those pictures which begin with the sound being taught and paste them inside the outline of that letter.

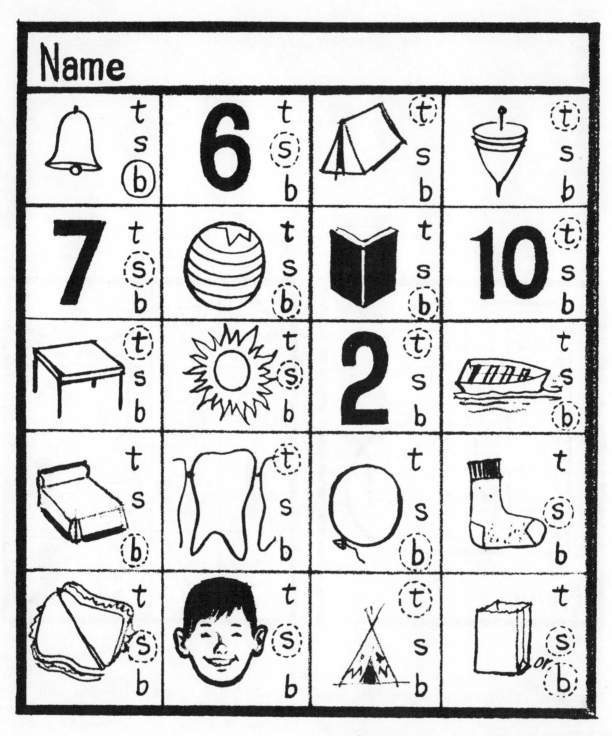

After the children have mastered the individual sounds, two or three may be combined on a check-test lesson such as this. The pictures should be named for the child and the correct sound circled at that time—or only circled with the finger and then marked again during an independent work period.

Initially no more than three sounds should be used on one sheet. Later, as skills develop, additional sounds may be added to the same lesson.

Name

_ucket	_ater	_ear	_ine
_ at	_ouse	_all	_ite
_ able	_etter	_even	_op
_alloon	_ish	_an	_un

After the children have mastered the ability to hear beginning consonant sounds and circle the correct sound when given a choice of letters, they should then be taught to name the pictures and supply the correct beginning sounds. At first the other letters of the word may be supplied, later a box may be provided and the children supply the correct sound without seeing the rest of the word.

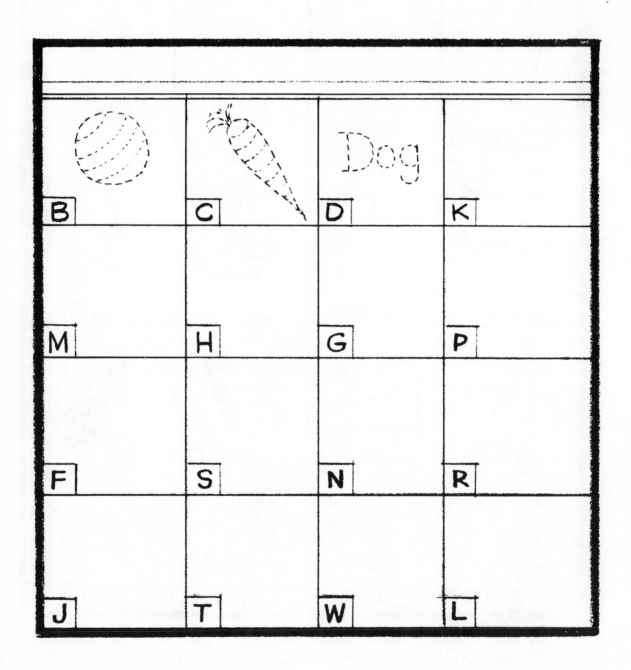

After the children hear sounds well enough, they may be asked to complete this type of exercise by providing either a picture or a word which begins with the sound in the box.

Name			
Play		Work	

To begin teaching the children how to classify things into groups, pictures provide an easily understood medium for nonreaders. Several lessons may precede the above lesson. In those earlier sessions, vocabulary-picture cards would be sorted according to verbal direction.

On this paper the children are taught only the two group-word names. Each picture is identified and the child independently pastes it under the correct word.

Pets		Toys	
dog	wagon	doll	bunny
ball	cat	playhouse	boat
pony	airplane	fish	bird

After children are able to classify pictures into groups, simple vocabulary words are introduced through the basic reading program. These words should be cut apart and pasted under the correct heading.

In some transition situations a *combination* of pictures and words may be used. Pictures *and* words are also useful at the earlier classification levels.

Things That Go	Things to Eat
a wagon	the car
lunch	birthday cake
a big train	a schoolbus
two red apples	breakfast
a sailboat	a big dinner
four cookies	scooter

Further practice in the ability to classify is gained through practice on lessons such as the one above. The word-phrases may either be cut out and pasted or written under the correct title.

Name

To Do	To Eat	To Play
_____	_____	_____
_____	_____	_____
_____	_____	_____
_____	_____	_____

jump	race	dinner	tag
apple	sing	sing	come
ball	cake	dolls	bread

To See	To Hear	To Ride In
_____	_____	_____
_____	_____	_____
_____	_____	_____
_____	_____	_____

book	train	man	wagon
mew	bang	bow-wow	colors
car	balloon	bus	zoom

Write the words under the correct title

The ability to classify is further developed by increasing the number of titles and the number and difficulty of the words to be classified.

Simple line drawings such as this series may be used to teach the earliest sequencing skills. The pictures should be mixed and placed on the chalk ledge or windowsill. The child must put them in the correct order. The teacher may tell the children a story about the pictures or they may make up their own.

Numbers 1, 2, 3 can be written on the chalkboard or taped to the windowsill if the teacher wishes to extend the concept to a numbered series.

47

This more advanced sequencing activity uses pictures along with the introduction of vocabulary and sequential numbering. To gradually increase difficulty, the bottom pictures may be mixed and fourth and fifth pictures added.

The number of pictures and the complexity of the vocabulary can be increased by making four boxes and then five pictures and sentences with the title preprinted in the first box. Then further increase the difficulty by using all six boxes.

Name

☐	Mother ate dinner with the children.
☐	The children came fast.
☐	Mother made dinner.
☐	Mother called the children.

Use 1-2-3-4 to put the story in order.

The most abstract and advanced level of sequencing is that which uses only words and numbers. On exercises of this type the children are expected to rearrange the entire story into its proper sequence by placing a number in the correct box. Three to six sentences may be used to vary the level of difficulty.

TEACHER MADE GAMES
AND DEVICES

front   reverse

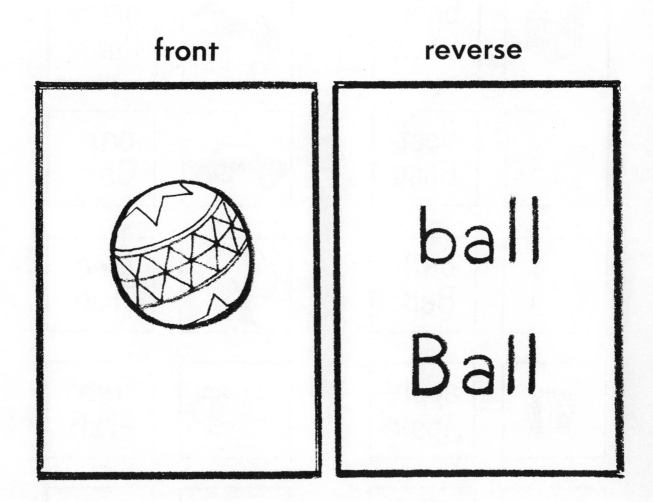

This is a reading circle or teacher and individual game which is designed to build sight vocabulary and check vocabulary already developed. Some 4″ x 6″ blank cards or pieces of white construction paper are used.

The cards may be set on the chalk ledge with the word side facing the children. Each child may point to a card, say the word, then turn it over to see if he is correct. If he is, he may keep the card.

For older children the front side may be placed facing them and they must spell the word correctly in order to keep the card. Alphabetizing may also be done with these cards.

On the next page are some examples of sight words which may be taught in this manner.

 pencil Pencil

 house House

 book Book

 horse Horse

 boat Boat

 car Car

 bell Bell

 tree Tree

 apple Apple

 fish Fish

 banana Banana

 cat Cat

 pear Pear

 run Run

54

money
Money

airplane
Airplane

cake
Cake

star
Star

candle
Candle

happy
Happy

hat
Hat

sad
Sad

cap
Cap

ice cream
Ice Cream

truck
Truck

wagon
Wagon

broom
Broom

chair
Chair

 table
Table

 bed
Bed

 cup
Cup

 flower
Flower

 mop
Mop

 bicycle
Bicycle

 boy
Boy

 in
In

 girl
Girl

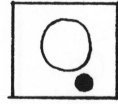 out
Out

 up
Up

 over
Over

 down
Down

 under
Under

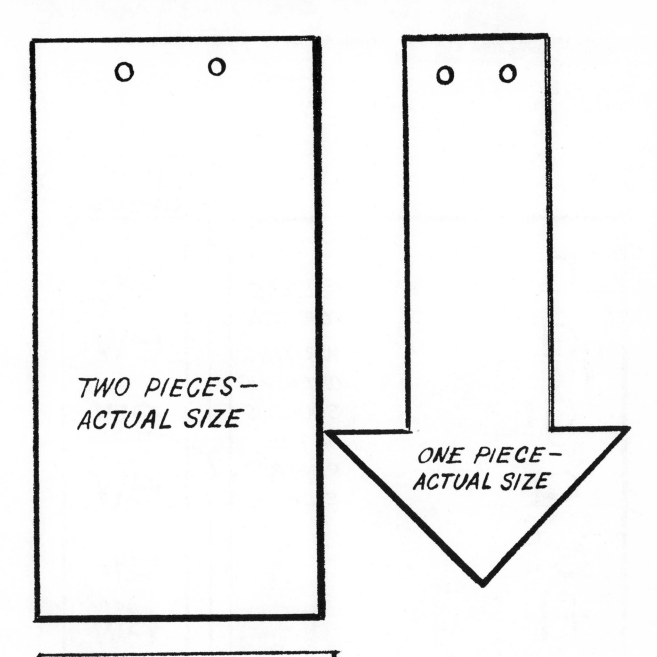

TWO PIECES—
ACTUAL SIZE

ONE PIECE—
ACTUAL SIZE

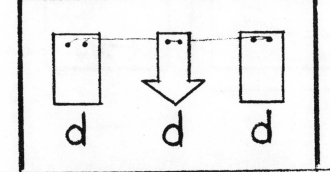

Example Words—Dog, dish, bed, middle, puddle, mud, day, head, do, cuddle, lady, winding, candy, poodle, etc.

This device is used for having the children show where they hear a sound in the word pronounced by the teacher. It is taped to the blackboard and the child slides the arrow on the string to the correct position.

Other sounds may be written in the three positions.

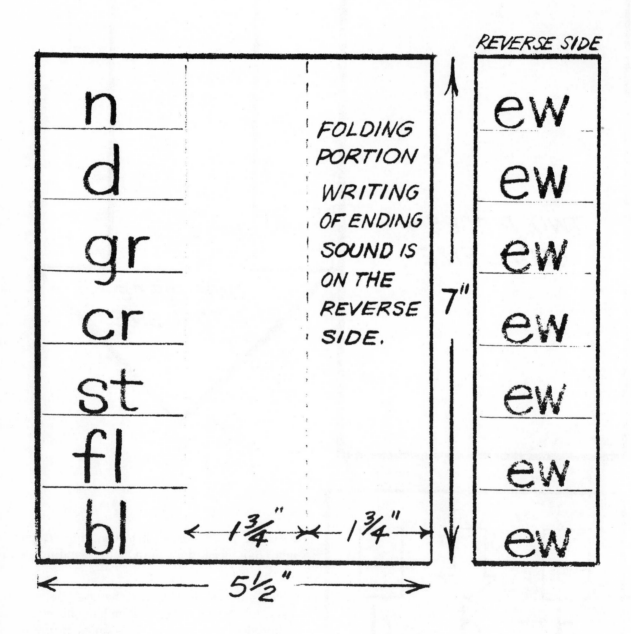

These folding cards provide the children with a manipulative device for practicing the blending of phonetic sound elements. After the sounds have been taught and are recognized in words, the chil-dren should be expected to work together or alone with these blending cards which are designed to teach them new words and build vocabulary pho-netically.

Folding Cards for Practicing Blending of Phonetic Sounds—7″ x 5½″ Tagboard

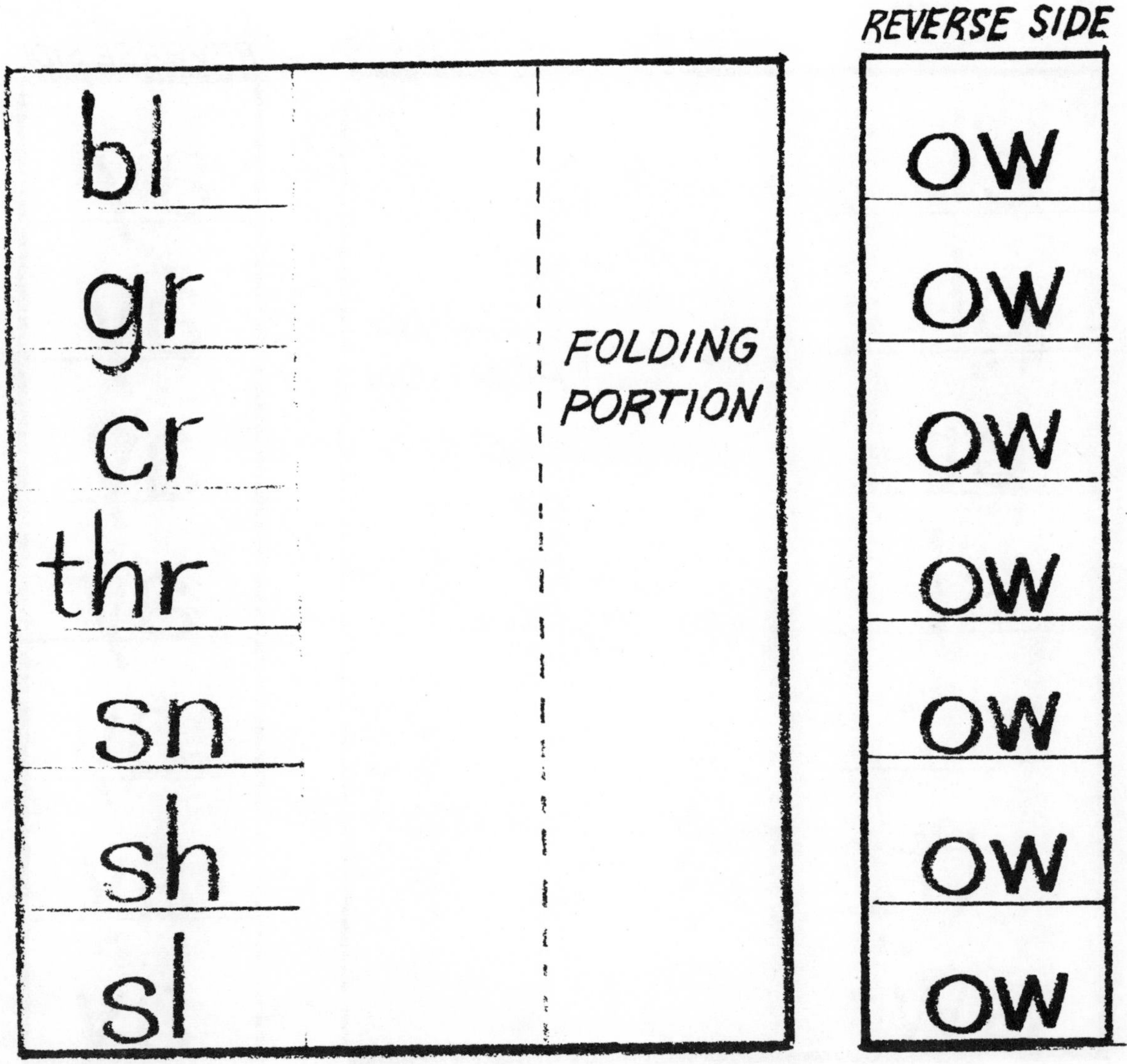
bl
gr
cr
thr
sn
sh
sl
FOLDING PORTION
REVERSE SIDE
ow
ow
ow
ow
ow
ow
ow

Folding Cards for Practicing Blending of Phonetic Sounds—7" x 5½" Tagboard

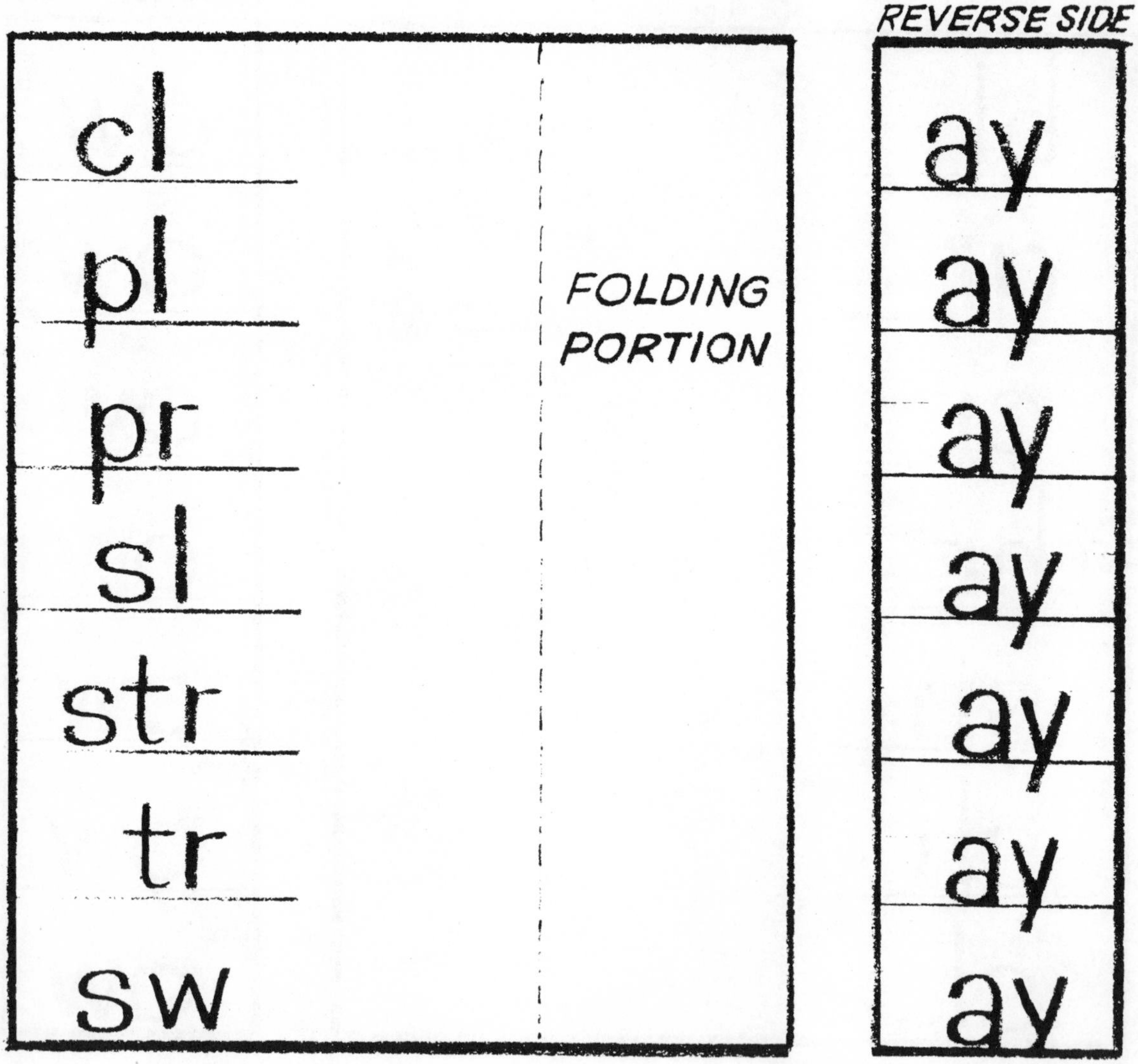

cl

pl

pr

sl

str

tr

sw

FOLDING
PORTION

REVERSE SIDE

ay

ay

ay

ay

ay

ay

ay

ay

Folding Cards for Practicing Blending of Phonetic Sounds—7" x 5½" Tagboard

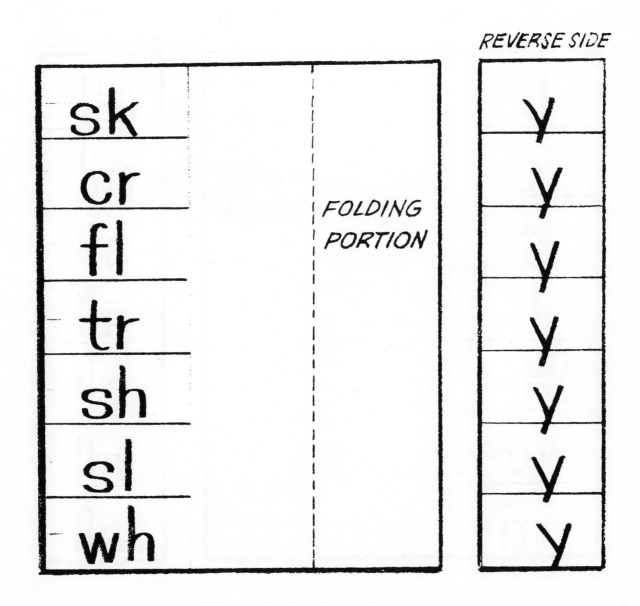

REVERSE SIDE

sk
cr
fl
tr
sh
sl
wh

FOLDING PORTION

y
y
y
y
y
y
y

Folding Cards for Practicing Blending of Phonetic Sounds—7" x 5½" Tagboard

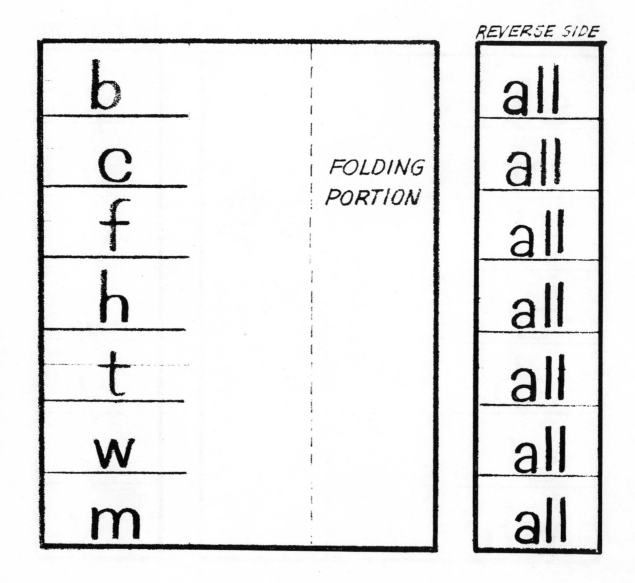

Folding Cards for Practicing Blending of Phonetic Sounds—7" x 5½" Tagboard

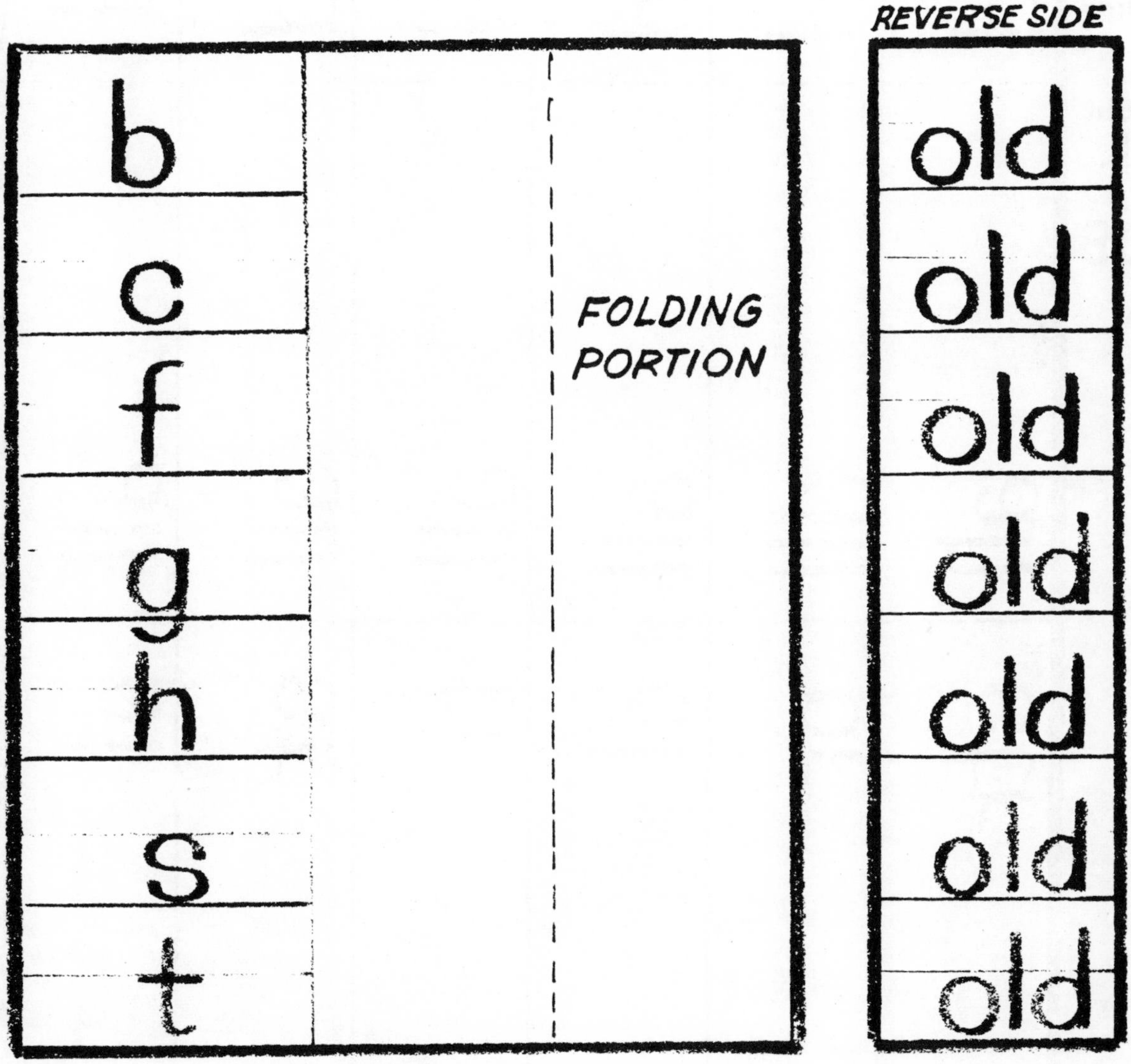

b		
c		
f		*FOLDING*
g		*PORTION*
h		
s		
t		

REVERSE SIDE

old
old
old
old
old
old
old
old

11 x7
3-way folding card for practice in the blending of phonetic sounds.

SIDE A

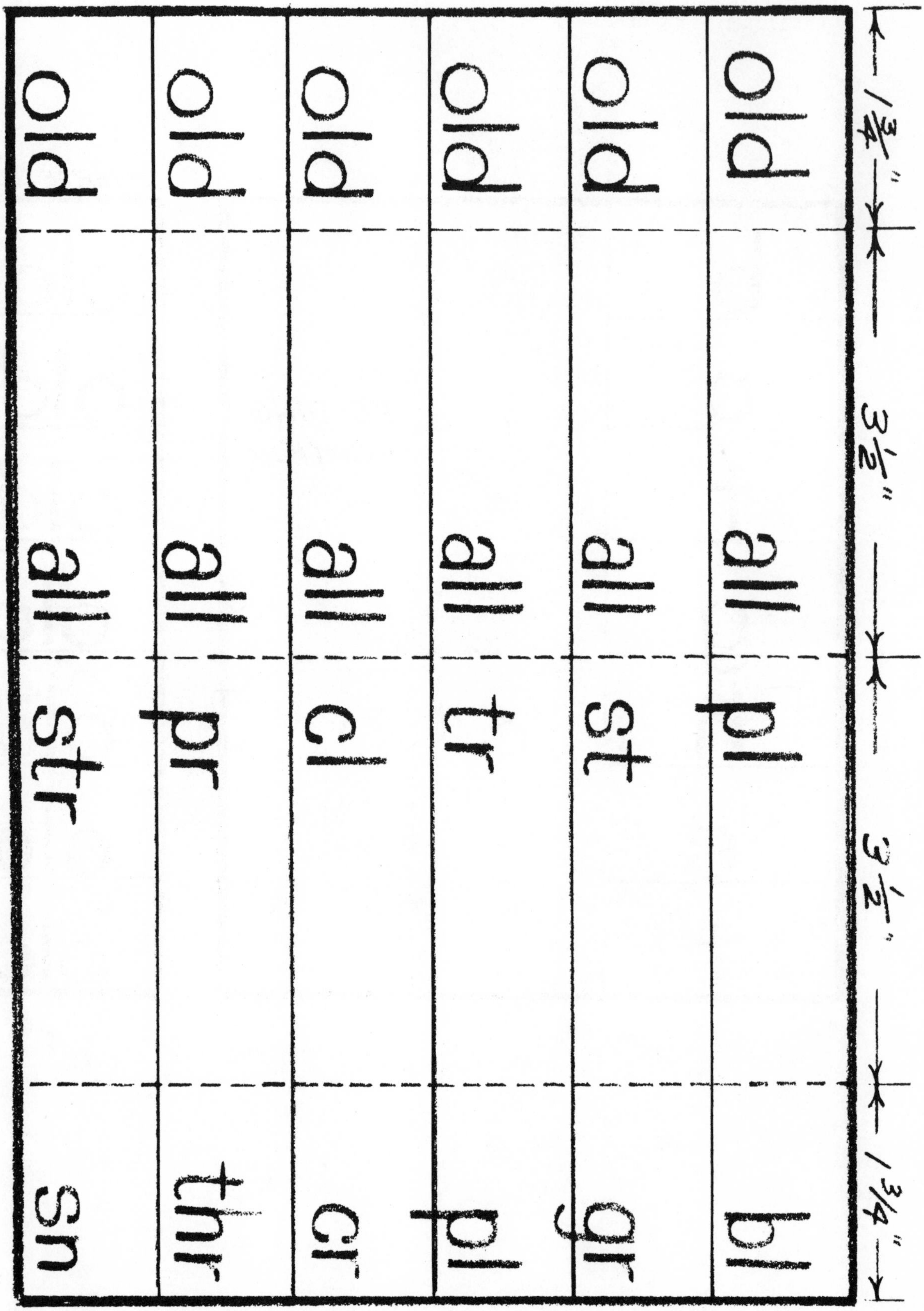

old	old	old	old	old	old
all	all	all	all	all	all
str	pr	cl	tr	st	pl
sn	thr	cr	pl	gr	bl

3/4"

3½"

3½"

1¾"

11 x7
3-way folding card for practice in the blending of phonetic sounds.

SIDE B

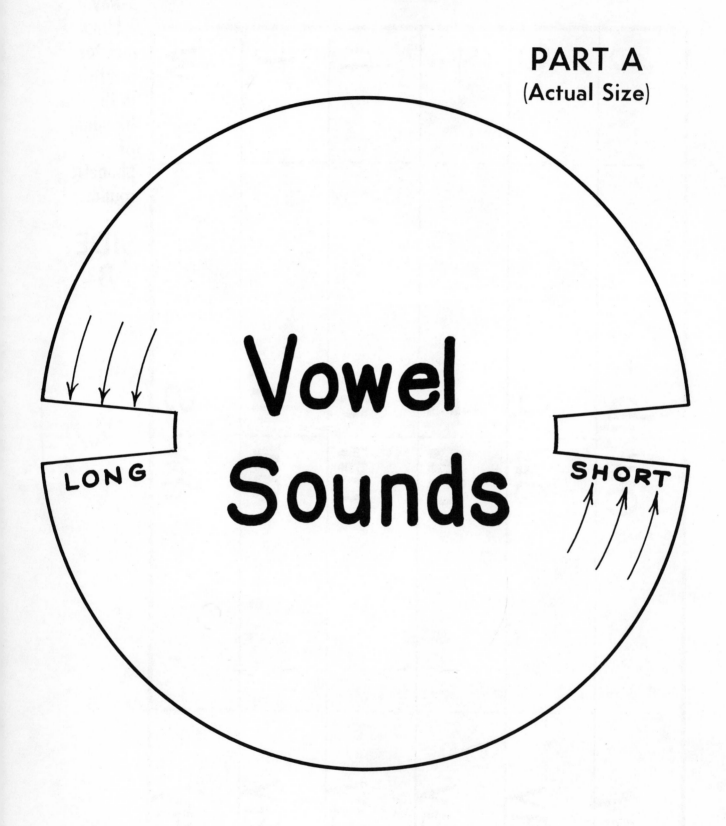

PART A
(Actual Size)

Long and Short Vowel Practice Wheel

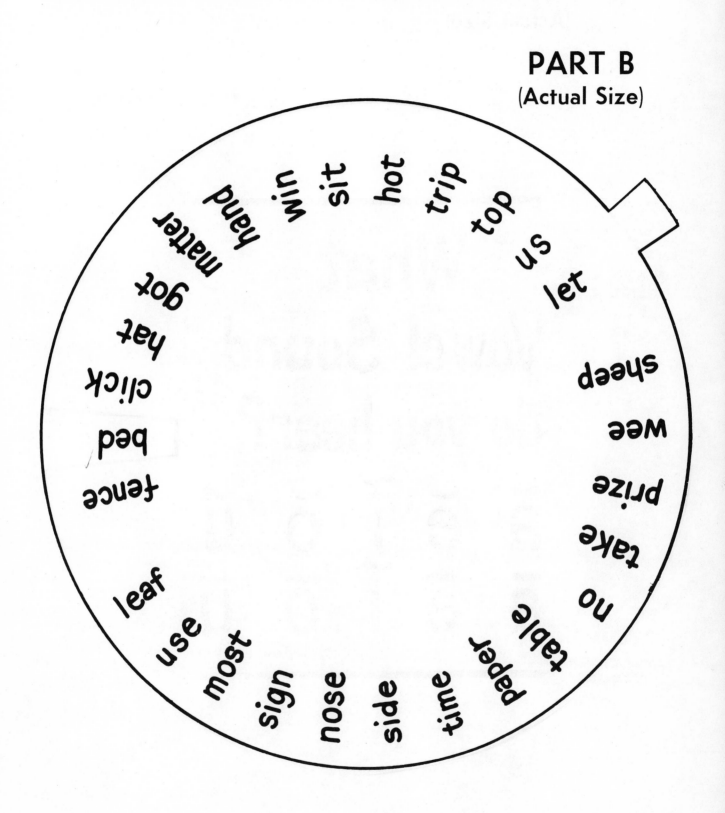

Practice wheel—PART A
(Actual Size)

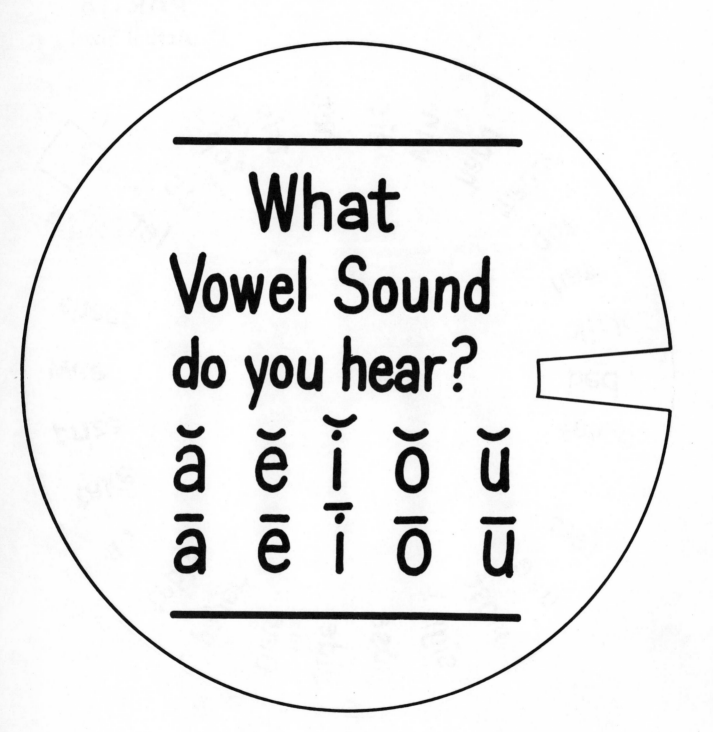

What
Vowel Sound
do you hear?

ă ĕ ĭ ŏ ŭ
ā ē ī ō ū

Practice wheel—PART B
(Actual Size)

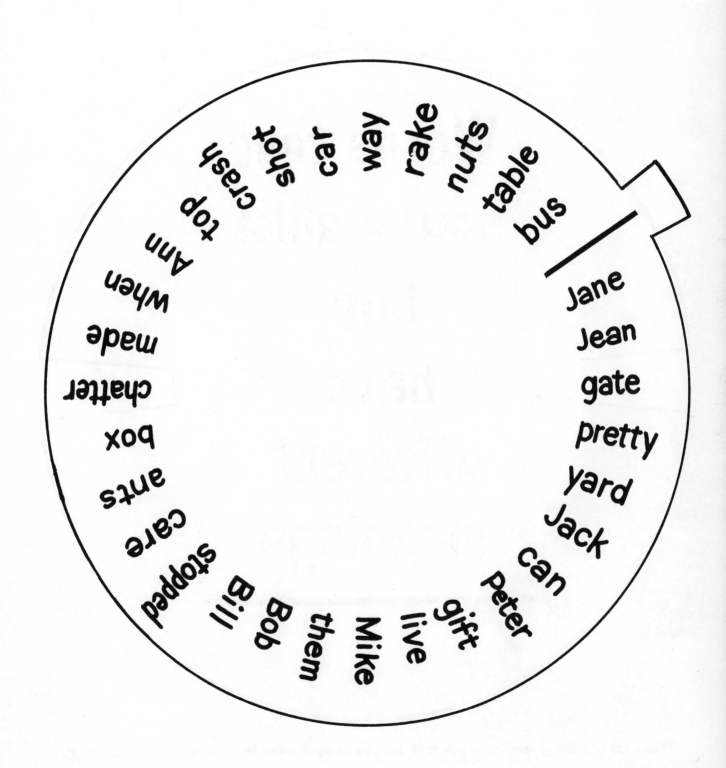

Cover–(Actual Size)
PART A

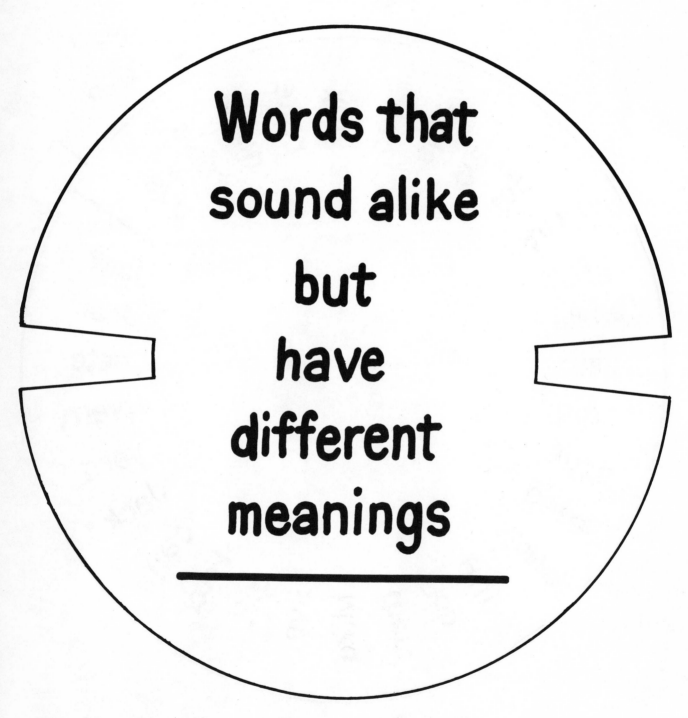

Words that sound alike but have different meanings

Device for practicing reading words that are pronounced alike but are unlike in meaning.

Words that sound alike—but have different meanings

PART B—BASE
(Actual Size)

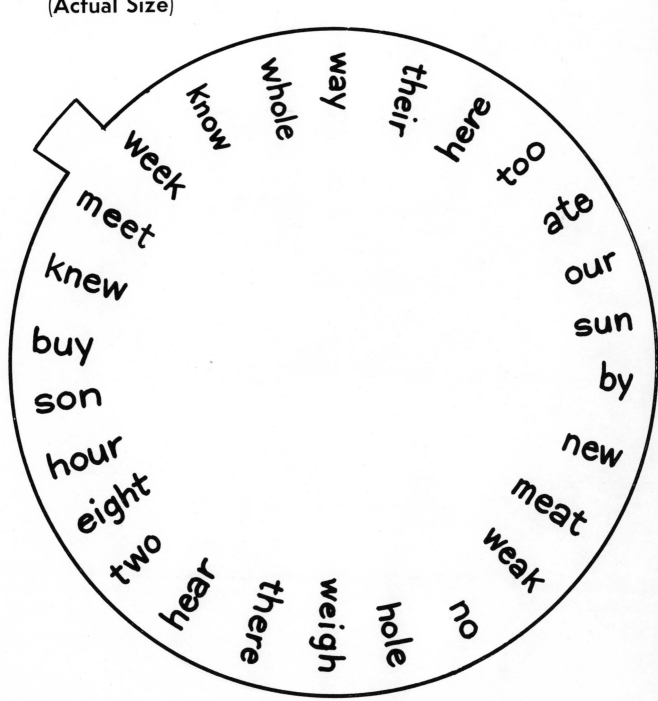

BULLETIN BOARDS

Go down reading river —

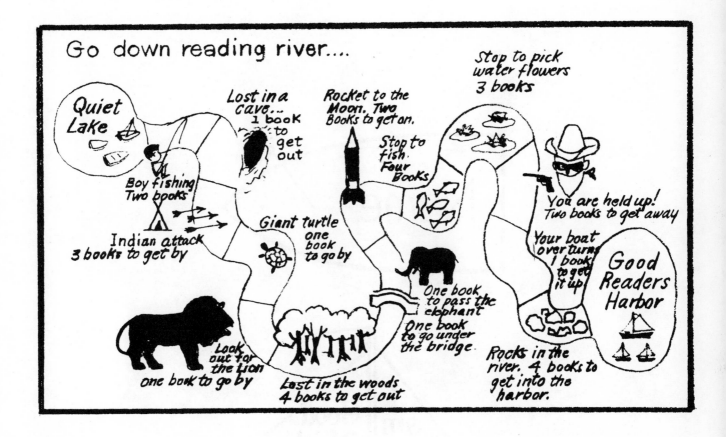

This reading progress bulletin board helps motivate the children to read from an individualized collection of books selected in advance by the teacher. A discussion of reading in general should be used to introduce the bulletin board. It should be pointed out that the person who does not read much is usually quiet and that each child will start out in a rowboat to go down the river, and then those that reach the Good Readers' Harbor will go back "up the river" in a sailboat. Many books are needed for this project (90-150).

The child may choose his books from the shelf or counter beneath this bulletin board. The next day he must be able to read a portion of the book orally to the teacher. The teacher may choose to have each child read to her each day; read to an-other child (a better reader), or select a few at random each day. It takes thirty books to "navigate" this river. Simplified versions or shorter charts may be used for younger children and beginning readers.

The "reading river" may be drawn on heavy white wrapping paper or made in sections for easy storage. If it is drawn with felt-tipped pens, an extra layer of paper should be rolled with it or placed between sections to prevent fading. Crayons are a good medium to use in preparing this bulletin board. Pictures may be cut out and pasted along the river if the teacher chooses not to draw them. Sample boat patterns appear on the next page.

BOATS FOR THE READING RIVER

These boats should be made of tagboard, file cards, or heavy construction paper.

The river should be three inches wide to provide for boats this size. It can be designed in an "up-and-down" manner and made more winding if space is limited in the classroom. When no wall space is available, the "river" may be reproduced in miniature and each child can color the water on an individual sheet as he progresses down the river. These individual sheets may be kept in a booklet or with the teacher.

BE A BOOKWORM—AND READ!

Actual
size
pieces
for the
children's
bookworms

←head

Paste
Head here

Name
(First Segment)

Paste

Name of
book read
(Title Segments)

Paste

Bookworms add a new segment each time a book is completed by the child. The teacher may require the child to read part of the book before adding a segment. Sometimes parents may verify on a check sheet that the child can read the book.

These bookworms make an interesting bulletin board, but when space is limited they can be taped to windowsills, door frames, desks, chalk ledge, or the wall.

This three-dimensional bulletin board is designed to create interest in books and the library in general. The title may be changed to any season and the small decorations around the cart and horse may be changed to fall leaves, snowflakes, or sunshine and toys. The horse may be made of tagboard by using an opaque projector to enlarge any picture of a horse or pony. Brown construction paper can be cut and folded to give the cart a "boxlike" effect. Large wheels (2) should be cut from construction paper or tagboard.

Book jackets should be borrowed from the library or paperback books (from one of the book clubs) pinned or stapled in the cart, around the cart, on the ground, etc. Whenever possible the same books should be made available to the children. This helps to stimulate their interest.

MISCELLANEOUS DEVICES

Window Bookmobiles for Progress Tabulating.

Each child uses an old box and decorates it like an old car. Slips with the titles of books read are put into the box-car. When five slips are collected they are removed and a star is pasted somewhere on the car. The slips are taken home after the star is affixed.

One colored star may be used—or several colors—using a different color for each of the five books.

This project can be simplified and the car reproduced on a ditto master and run on construction paper. A slit may be cut for inserting the book slips.

The cars may be kept on windowsills, the bulletin board, or in the children's desks.

A book mobile may be made for each child to tally and record books read by each child. This device is especially useful in rooms with limited display area. Each "book jacket" miniature can be made of construction paper and several may be dittoed at one time. Gummed notebook rein-forcements are excellent for reinforcing the area around the punched holes. Jackets are fastened together with either thread or string.

The book mobiles can be fastened to ceiling light brackets or thumbtacked into acoustical tile ceilings.

I have
finished this
whole book. I can
read it at home.
Help me to
remember to take
it back on the next
morning I have school.

Thank You.

 *Relax and listen!*

When the children complete a book in a basic series, we make a "cover" similar to this in order to:

1. Remind parents the book must come back to school.

2. Avoid ridicule of the level of reader by other children.

3. Protect the book.

This parent-education booklet is designed to be simple and to the point. The pages may be made with line drawings on a single ditto master.

The four pages may be cut apart with a paper cutter, or by the children. Construction-paper covers may be dittoed or lettered by either the teacher or the children.

Two or three staples will fasten the booklet together.

1. Be a good
   listener.

2. Relax and
   show interest.

3. Read to him,
   too.

4. Praise him
   when he makes
   progress.

SUMMARY

Teaching reading to mentally retarded children requires the use of special techniques. The ways in which mental retardation affects the learning process of reading must be completely understood by the teacher and curriculum author. Each reading area must be explored in detail to evaluate it in terms of the needs of the mentally retarded.

Each area of the reading programs used in special-education classes is analyzed in terms of the needs of the children for whom the program is designed. The school program and the teaching of reading using various methods of instruction must be carefully correlated.

Instructional procedures which may be used to individualize reading programs and stimulate learning should be included in the special-education reading program. Instructional methodology must be varied, but carefully planned, to insure systematic and sequential learning.

The reading needs of the trainable child are few for their life expectancies in our society. Their training is basically the same as the readiness program given to the educable mentally retarded children.

Materials for teaching reading in the special class are perhaps the most important part of the instruction in reading. The materials section is meant only to guide teachers to try new methods and devices to stimulate the interests and abilities of the children in the class.